OLD LOCHGELLY
by
RHONA WILSON

Participants in one of Lochgelly's West End Picnics. Another picture of the parade shows people holding decorated placards reading 'Aye Mind The Bairns'.

© Stenlake Publishing 1998
First published in the United Kingdom, 1998
by Stenlake Publishing, Ochiltree Sawmill, The Lade,
Ochiltree, Ayrshire, KA18 2NX
Telephone / Fax: 01290 423114

ISBN 1 84033 022 8

ACKNOWLEDGEMENTS

I'd like to thank the staff of Lochgelly Library who were very helpful during my research, and also Mr Jimmy Robertson who talked to me about life in Lochgelly and read over my completed manuscript. Thanks to Eric Eunson and John Band for supplying additional information and pictures.

The publishers would like to thank Eileen Watt who made her collection of Lochgelly pictures available for use in the book, and also supplied additional information. The pictures on page 7 and the back cover are reproduced by courtesy of Jim Kinnell; those on the inside front and back covers are by courtesy of John Band; the picture on page 21 is by courtesy of Eric Eunson.

THE PUBLISHERS REGRET THAT THEY CANNOT SUPPLY
COPIES OF ANY PICTURES FEATURED IN THIS BOOK.

FURTHER READING

Rev. Andrew Murray, *Statistical Account of Scotland*, 1790-1791
Rev Andrew Murray, *New Statistical Account of Scotland*, 1833
Alex Westwater, *Third Statistical Account of Scotland*, 1946-1949
Central Fife Times; *Dunfermline Press*; *Dunfermline Journal*
Fifeshire Directory 1888-1889, pub. Charles Lamburn
Lochgelly: The Official Guide, pub. Burgh Council (pre-1975)
David A. Allan, *There Was a Happy Land: Lochgelly FC 1890-1928*
A. Cunningham, *Mining in the Kingdom*, John Orr, 1913
Ed. M. Docherty, *Auld Bob Selkirk*, 1996 (no pub. details)
A.H. Millar, *Fife: Pictorial and Historical*, A Westwood & Son, 1895
John Pinder, *Autobiography of a Private Soldier*, 1841, Simpkin et al.
Glen L. Pride, *The Kingdom of Fife*, RIAS, 1990
T.C. Smout, *A Century of the Scottish People*, Fontana Press, 1987
Alex Westwater's Lochgelly, Alex Westwater Memorial Trust, 1994

The 1938 Empire Exhibition was held in Glasgow to raise morale and give a boost to industry both locally and nationally. As well as an extravaganza of themed pavilions in Bellahouston Park, its various entertainments included a football tournament, and this Lochgelly crowd were photographed after the final. A crowd of 82,000 watched Celtic beat Everton, Crum scoring the winning goal in extra time. Celtic captain William Lyon was presented with the trophy, a miniature replica of the Tower of Empire, the principal landmark of the Bellahouston site.

INTRODUCTION

Lochgelly's early origins are vague. A Celtic Horresti tribe is thought to have given the loch its name, rooted in the word *gile* and meaning 'the white and shining water'. Some Victorian historians, however, prefer a more romantic-sounding etymology which translates as 'wild moorland populated by gypsies'. That the village existed in 1485 is known by references to it in charters of the time; it is also documented in the Wemyss family papers of the early 1580s. In the late eighteenth century its coal was held cheap, referred to by the writer of the Statistical Account of Scotland (1790-1791) as a phenomenon more than an industry. 'It is to be dug', he said, 'in every corner of the parish, and scarcely exceeds a farthing a stone at the pit mouth.' A rural backwater, Lochgelly had neither political nor industrial significance until it began to mine this casually-regarded resource and rapidly developed both.

Despite the abundance of coal, mining in Lochgelly was still relatively undeveloped as late as the 1830s, although with just 74 miners the Cluny Colliery was one of the largest employers in the district. When Lochgelly's industrialists decided to go into large-scale production in the mid-nineteenth century it was iron rather than coal that they chose to exploit, obtaining a lease to mine ironstone on the Lochgelly Estate in 1851. This industry collapsed in the 1860s when imports of cheap Spanish ore made ironstone mining uneconomical. The railway system which had been put in place in the late 1840s to facilitate it, however, proved a solid basis for developing an alternative industry and in 1872 the Lochgelly Iron Company became the Lochgelly Iron and Coal Company, five years after its blast furnaces stopped operating.

The opening of Lochgelly railway station in 1849 meant that the town's coal could be distributed at a time when industrial as well as domestic users were beginning to depend on it. Once it began, the development of Lochgelly as a mining town was rapid. Formerly a part of Auchterderran Parish, the mid-nineteenth century saw it erected into a parish in its own right as its population increased. By 1877 it had been elevated to a Police Burgh, a measure often taken by expanding towns since a burgh's tax-raising powers provided it with the finances to improve public services. The mid-1890s saw further industrial activity in the area. Two pits were sunk at the Minto Colliery in Brigghills and Lochgelly's Mary Pit was re-sunk to reach its deepest workable seams.

The speed of the mining industry's expansion certainly had some disadvantages. The sudden abundance of work led to a rapid influx of incomers from Ireland, Lanarkshire and the Lothians, the latter group perceived as politically radical. Aside from the fact that they had to be close to the mines, little thought was given to how these miners should be housed. Nearby settlements such as Glencraig – isolated and lacking facilities – quickly acquired a reputation as 'rough'. It's little wonder that when the mines closed settlements such as this were abandoned; the 'ghost town' of Glencraig is a case in point. The biggest problem with Lochgelly's boom, however, was its dependence on a single industry.

In 1905 the introduction of the first conveyor belt transport systems and mechanised coal-cutters hinted at what was to come and the consequences of it. Lochgelly's pit ponies were the first casualties of an industry which was becoming capital- as opposed to labour-intensive; they had become surplus to requirements by 1932. In addition to economic pressure from the gas, electricity and nuclear power industries, mechanisation had a significant effect on the lifetime of the coal industry. In the 1950s Lochgelly's coal industry was still expected to have several decades of life left in it, but just ten years later technology had developed to the extent that seventy-odd men could produce 1,500 tons of coal in a day, a task which formerly took hundreds. The National Coal Board reduced its life expectancy for Lochgelly's pits to just a few years, the Scottish Office abandoning plans for a new town in the area accordingly. One by one Lochgelly's pits closed.

Today the town is surviving the loss of its main industry, despite being slightly the worse for wear. Unlike Glencraig, Lochgelly was well enough established not to disappear completely, and in the past couple of decades there have been signs of regeneration. The Lochgelly Centre, a massive recreation and education facility, was opened by Prince Philip in 1976. A few years previous to this Lochore Meadows Country Park opened on wasteland reclaimed from the mining industry. Opencast mining at Muirhead was touted as a saviour in recent years and some employment is provided at the nearby Mossmorran petrochemical complex. Despite the lack of employment opportunities within its burgh boundaries, the railway which kick-started the iron and mining industries is just as economically important today. Lochgelly station provides a commuter link to Edinburgh, and the variety of occupations and opportunities it offers.

Lochgelly Main Street. Historical accounts of Lochgelly's appearance differ. One local worthy recalled that its roads were piled high on either side with 'evil-smelling mud and horse manure' whereas a turn of the century historian informed his readers approvingly that it '[boasted] the possession of a main street, elegant private residences in considerable numbers and commodious public buildings of much architectural beauty'. Miners only began to live in the town around the mid-nineteenth century which suited their predecessors, the weavers, just fine; serfs until 1799, colliers had little status and commanded even less respect. Despite the many local pits, Lochgelly has suffered surprisingly little subsidence on account of ancient feu laws. Under these the landowner could be held responsible for damage done to property by coal workings, so the Earl of Minto had a particular incentive to ensure that pits were sunk outwith the burgh boundaries.

Main Street, Lochgelly

Outwith Lochgelly's burgh boundaries it was a different story altogether. Acres became waterlogged as land near the River Ore subsided; the town's *extended* boundaries (there were four extensions in a fifty year period) were not protected under the original feus. The last extension, to take in the area of South Street and Cooper Ha' Park, was agreed at a meeting of the Town Council in 1946 and went against the wishes of central government. With involvement in other proposed local house-building projects, the Department of Health wanted the council to hold off. Lochgelly authorities had little faith in the plans, however, and Bailie Gordon pointed out that the Department had committed nothing to paper. Also, since a brake on house-building had been applied in nearby towns, places for Lochgelly residents in the Department's new town would necessarily be restricted.

Tram lines, absent in this picture, made their exit c.1936. The row of cottages on the south side of Main Street (visible on the previous page) survived until after the Second World War. This picture shows the block as it stands today, with new flats above modern shop units. In terms of building the turn of the century was Lochgelly's boom-time, with the coal company trying to match its employees' demands for accommodation. Despite efforts, there was never enough and the town's three lodging houses were always full. Almost none of the 300-odd but and bens in the village c.1870 are standing today. Despite local authority building there was still a housing shortage in the 1950s and Lochgelly's increasingly fragile economic situation made private builders reluctant to invest in the town.

This tongue-in-cheek postcard with its message to 'sign the pledge' refers to the Scottish temperance movement of the early twentieth century. Scotland's east coast had its own particular approach to the evils of alcohol. 'Gothenburg' pubs were run by the temperance societies, their aim to provide a safe environment for the moderate consumption of alcohol, with profits ploughed back into the community. In 1790 Lochgelly had six inns, supported by the village's annual markets, where a festival spirit was usually in evidence. By the 1830s this number had risen to twelve, the minister of the time lamenting that, 'drunkenness, formerly rare, is now . . . frequent'. Whisky smuggled in from the Highlands was blamed for the increase, but ministerial warnings didn't improve the situation. Fife's 1888-1889 trade directory listed twenty alcohol dealers, fourteen of them located in Lochgelly. When the Forbes Mackenzie Act restricted the hours during which alcohol could be sold some businesses went underground. Two churchwarden pipes crossed in a window was apparently a well-known sign in the district for advertising a shebeen, an illegal drinking den.

Macainsh Parish Church lies just out of shot to the right. In 1861 the minister of Lochgelly Parish Church (visible on page 13) was Dr Mair, a man of some humour and thoughtfulness. One of his elders, his autobiography assures us proudly, had a dream before his appointment in which Dr Mair appeared as the new minister, a superstitious story he seems to have enjoyed. Miners living in the town didn't take a shine to him though and made certain to lock up their houses and turn the lights off when he did his round of nightly visits. One drunken miner threatened to throw himself down a pit unless the minister gave him a sixpence; another on being asked why he worked hard and then wasted the money on drink replied, 'Do you think I would work so hard if it werena to get the drink?' Despite it all, Mair made an effort to understand. He got Andrew Landale, manager of the coal company, to give him a tour of a mine (in disguise) which profoundly affected him: 'At every movement the back going against the hard, relentless rock above caused an inexpressible feeling of helplessness. For once in my life . . . I think I knew what utter despair [was]'.

Lochgelly's Miners' Welfare Institute opened in 1925 amidst mob scenes. A 200-strong crowd stormed the opening ceremony, led by eight delegates which the Institute's committee refused to recognise because they had been elected by the radical Reform Union. One of them, Jimmie Stewart, led the crowd into the building with the order 'Don't destroy any property because it's ours!', which he delivered from the librarian's counter. Mr Paul, Managing Director of the coal company, suggested that Lochgelly's miners made a financial contribution to the Institute if they wanted a say in the way it was run, adding that he considered this condition to be 'the reasonable request of a gentleman'. Eventually, he conceded to negotiations with the delegates behind closed doors. Afterwards an immediate meeting in the public park to elect eight representatives was announced, at which the Reform Union's men were duly elected. A Mr Crooks, freshly elected, graciously accepted the hall on behalf of the workers of Lochgelly.

Lochgelly's West End picnic, with Mrs Whyte at the head of the parade (other members of the Whyte family appear in the picture as children). Holidays were rare (and certainly unpaid) until well into the twentieth century. In the 1790s Lochgelly miners had just one holiday a year, known as Handsel-Monday, during which they had family get-togethers. Summer day-trips like this one were consequently highly valued, and big turnouts ensured they were community events. When they took over the coal industry in 1946 the National Coal Board apparently made veiled threats to miners in the local press, in case any were considering not turning up for work during the festive season. The NCB announced that the reason there would be no penalties for absence on New Years' Day was that it trusted the men to turn up. Rumours had been going around that many miners would take this as a holiday because of the new paid leave conditions, leaving the pits idle.

One of Lochgelly's most famous institutions was its tawse shop, established in the 1870s and situated at the east end of Main Street. Mr Robert Philip was a saddler and ironmonger when his son David was a pupil teacher at the Lochgelly Iron and Coal Company School. David Philip later went on to study teaching at college and took with him a tawse his father had fashioned to provide him with a little assistance. It was so effective that word of mouth recommendations began to draw in many orders to the shop, the Lochgelly 'belt' eventually so popular that Philip's took on two apprentices. One of them, James Heggie, took over the business after his boss died and later sold it to the other, Mr Dick. The Dick family still owned the Main Street shop in the 1970s when, even though corporal punishment had been banned in some schools, the tawse was still popular – I wonder with whom exactly! In the mid-seventies the original premises were sold and the business moved to Cowdenbeath.

This picture shows the junction of Main Street and Bank Street. The Co-op butchery opened in 1884 but has long since been demolished to open up the Cross. Lochgelly earned a reputation for political radicalism in the past, with Jimmie Stewart of the Institute demonstration one of the town's foremost political players. Stewart was one of the first communist councillors in Fife and was also involved in the earliest secret delegations sent to Russia by Britain after the 1917 Revolution. As a Town Bailie and ever politically aware, his style of sentencing maddened more conventional councillors. On sentencing two men for fighting he pronounced, 'Admonished and I would like to tell you that the people you should be fighting are the capitalists.'

Bank Street cuts off the east end of Lochgelly's Main Street and wasn't developed until the 1890 to 1910 period, although it is now a substantial thoroughfare. North Street, which is part of the way down it at the post office, was at the very edge of town when it was first created. The group on the left are squatting outside Alex Westwater's printers' shop. Westwater was born in Bank Street in 1875 and eventually took over his father's publishing and printing business, issuing the 'Lochgelly Times' as well as several of the postcards printed in this book. His shop was popular on Saturday nights when men gathered outside to wait for the day's sports news which came in around five or six o'clock. Before the advent of television and radio these hastily printed sheets of around eight pages in length were the fastest means of getting the news. Westwater was conferred the unusual status of Honorary Burgess for services to the town some time before his death in 1960.

Bank Street before the advent of the Cinema de Luxe and the rebuilding of St Andrew's Parish Church. Earning a living from mining was harsh, not only for men, but for the women who worked underground until this practice was banned in 1832. The parish minister of the 1790s cited bad diet and dark, cold and dirty homes as particular trials, commenting that, 'The amount of food a labourer consumes is unequal to the energy he expends'. Each of the eight miners in Sir Gilbert Elliot's first pit was assisted by his wife, who carried coal to the pit-head in a basket on her back. Female labour was poorly valued, women labourers of the 1830s getting only 50% of male wages. Even so, male wages, particularly those of miners, were afflicted by regular deductions. A wage slip for a Lochgelly Coal Company employee of the 1900s showed a list of possible deductions as follows: for tool sharpening, explosives, materials, medical fees, Nurse Association, hospital, Carlow House, ambulance waggon, Friendly Society, Welfare Institute, baths and bands.

Lochgelly's Jenny Gray pit and Dundonald pit had both closed by 1964, with further closures in neighbouring districts. Local businesses were feeling the pinch but Mr Timmons, manager of the Cinema de Luxe and eternal optimist, was unperturbed, choosing that year to expand his business. The Luxe was closed down for a few weeks for modifications so that it could offer wrestling matches and dancing in addition to movies and bingo. 'The position cannot get much worse,' Timmons asserted in the *Dunfermline Press*, 'things can only improve.' In short, he was wrong. Today the Luxe is still standing but only just. No. 28 Bank Street (now the Style Salon) was once a cafe with a connecting door to the cinema foyer. The Buttercup Dairy, Keir's shoe shop and Sam Stewart's bicycle shop were opposite the cinema. The van on the right was driven by Bert Stewart who worked for John Clark the baker.

BANK ST, LOCHGELLY.

Lochgelly's Minto Hotel once had stables round the back for its guests; some thirty years ago it ceased to offer accommodation and became a bar. The onset of the First World War heralded uncertainty for the town's miners and their families. Pits were put on short time and the relief agencies were quickly called in as families floundered on two-day week wages. Lochgelly miners were lucky in the first instance, as few changes were made to their working hours, although the situation could be predicted no more than one week ahead. 1,000-odd men from the town had left for the war by November 1914. The Police Courts noted a decrease in cases of petty crimes and drunkenness and Lochgelly's streets, minus a male presence, seemed eerily quiet. Both abroad and at home the situation seemed perilous, and this was reflected in church attendances; a communion service at the parish church in November 1914 had the highest attendance on record.

Shopkeepers experienced immediate difficulties in obtaining supplies, especially basics like eggs, butter and sugar. Whilst wholesale prices for these had risen by some 15 to 20%, traders were held to a 5% increase in the prices they charged. Britain's coal industry was particularly vulnerable to wartime conditions since it relied so heavily on its export trade. The big fear was that if the passage to neutral ports was threatened the pits would be closed down entirely. Of all Lochgelly's businesses the large Co-operative store showed the healthiest profit margins; this boded well for the town since it accounted for a large proportion of Lochgelly's trading. Andrew Mathieson's Railway Tavern occupied the corner of the tenement on the right for many years. The land beside it was once a putting green used by miners, but was earmarked as part of the site for the new post office just prior to the Second World War.

A later picture with the new post office in place. At the start of the First World War some commentators were reasonably optimistic that the hostilities would not last too long. An article expressing Canadian opinion appeared in the *Dunfermline Journal* in mid-November 1914 stating the government's hope that, 'a few months will mercifully see the end of the war and a restoration of peace', before going on to extol Canada's virtues as a place to live and work. Readers were assured that there would be a rush to emigrate after the war just as there had been after the Franco-Prussian war of the 1870s. What was wanted were farmers who would stay and settle on the land instead of exploiting immigration policies. The country had been plagued by 'wheat miners' in the past – speculators who bought cheap acres under immigration deals and sold them for a large profit after the stipulated occupation period, sowing wheat crops in the meantime. Dunfermline was targeted for adverts such as this because of its strong agricultural tradition although, ironically, it was the miners who emigrated in their droves after the 1921 and 1926 General Strikes.

Lochgelly's Co-operative Society developed from small beginnings to become one of the town's foremost businesses. Its first meetings were held in 1865 at the village hall in Hall Street, later labelled the 'Society's Hall' on maps. From a single store in Main Street with just one member of staff it developed into an employer of hundreds with large premises in Bank Street and branches scattered throughout the surrounding mining settlements. The feu beside the Minto Hotel, where its buildings still stand today, was taken up in 1887. A large bakery was built first of all, with grocery and drapery departments added as the society prospered in the early 1890s. Co-ops were largely set up to offer an alternative to coal company truck shops (so called from the French word *troquer*, to barter) which often offered poor-quality goods at high prices, but also brought down some local traders. In 1926 Mr Reid, who had a grocer's shop in Minto Street, had to sell out to the Co-op during the General Strike because of Lochgelly's dire economic situation.

These buildings originally housed the Co-op's grocery and drapery departments but were later converted to reading and recreation rooms. The Co-op suffered three disastrous fires in its history. In 1910, only seven years after being built, the Bank Street/Chapel Street premises almost entirely burned down. Two boys raised the alarm one evening at 9 p.m. for what was, to begin with, a very small fire. Poor planning and crowd control seems to have exacerbated the situation. Doors and windows were forced open, ventilating the fire which had initially been confined to a mattress on the ground floor. Members of the crowd got in the way of the firemen, and also managed to break the main water hydrant in their eagerness to help. The Buckhaven fire engine, when it finally arrived, had to fight its way along Bank Street which was crowded with an estimated 10,000 spectators. Some had ulterior motives and there was a spate of looting as the night went on, concentrated in the Co-op's millinery department and store rooms and at the neighbouring Minto Hotel. By about 10 p.m. the roof had fallen in; the town clock collapsed a little earlier as it chimed 9.45. The Buckhaven team worked through the night and managed to save parts of the building including the van shed and the granary. At an emergency meeting held the next day it was decided to convert the reading room into a grocery store, and a special train laden with a whole new stock of provisions was laid on the following Monday morning.

Just three years later, in 1913, the Co-op burned down again. Lochgelly's elevated situation meant that the fire could be seen for miles around and an estimated 20,000 turned out to see the blaze. This time there wasn't any water to begin with because of town policy. At the time Lochgelly's water supply was cut off overnight to conserve water, and even once it was connected the pressure was inadequate. The Buckhaven Fire Brigade were called for again, suffering some accidents on their own account before they'd even had time to roll out a hose. Firemaster Thompson was thrown from the van on a sharp turn *en route* to Lochgelly and James Wallace, jumping off the engine before it had stopped moving, got a crushed foot for his pains. This time the firefighting was more successful, with various workshops and the whole west wing saved. Since half the town turned out to spectate the pits were plagued by non-attendance the next day; the Jenny Gray was closed for almost the whole day. This picture shows the damage after the Co-op fire of 1910.

BANK STREET, LOCHGELLY

Bank Street's replacement Co-op building, now crumbling and coated in moss. Most of the building is boarded up although there is a small Co-op supermarket in the ground floor with a branch of Shoefayre next to it. Its grandiose style is described disparagingly as 'florid' by one architectural writer. The building certainly does look overblown by today's standards and is a world apart even from the utilitarian designs of the twenties just ten years after it was built.

Bank Street, Lochgelly

Co-ops were just one means of combating poverty in the past. In the eighteenth century penny weddings were held with guests donating money towards furniture to help the couple set up home. Surprisingly, these were frowned upon by some ministers who preached sermons criticising the practice. Charity certainly had an ambivalent status, begrudged by those who gave it and received in shame by those who needed it. In the 1790s Lochgelly had just 22 people listed on the monthly poor roll. By the 1830s this group were still financed by the interest on the lump sum from church collections although resources were dwindling because of a decrease in interest rates. The alternative – an assessment (tax) on the local heritors – was avoided to maintain their goodwill, and was only levied three times over a forty year period. Lochgelly parish tended to award money for one-off occurrences such as sickness and accidents as opposed to regular maintenance payments.

The building on the left in front of the Co-op was originally Lochgelly's police station. Around 1760 the town was the site of a famous gypsy encampment and its muir, later covered by coal company houses, was one of the chief meeting places for gypsies in central Scotland. The local community held them in no great favour, a local ditty called *The Lochgelly Gypsies* detailing exactly why: 'A plundering race/ Still eager to invade/ On spoil they lived/ And made of theft a trade.' The authorities made no attempt to dispel these ideas. One of the Lochgelly gypsies' long-term leaders, Charlie Graham, was hanged at Perth while Nan Broon, a well-known fighter, was whipped through the streets of Aberdeen. Auchterderran's Statistical Account of the 1790s stated that two had been banished within the previous six years. The gypsies survived at Lochgelly until the loss of the common muir to house-building projects, such as the 'Happyland' tenements, and the arrival of pits including the nearby Jenny Gray.

This Bank of Scotland branch (formerly an office of the Union Bank), has been knocked down and rebuilt in the same place. The mansion house to the left was once used as accommodation for bankers and is now a lawyer's office. A savings bank was mentioned by Lochgelly's minister of the 1830s who seems to have operated it along with another minister in the town. Most of the depositors were working-class and the ministers were responsible for lodging their savings at the Kirkcaldy branch of the Bank of Scotland. Friendly Societies were another important self-help measure before the advent of the Welfare State; they provided their members with funds in cases of injury or illness. Lochgelly's first was the Lochgelly Benefit Society, which was set up in 1830 and later became a Funeral Society, death itself being another potentially unbearable expense. Even in the 1950s some of these old organisations, such as the Ancient Order of Free Gardeners and the Foresters, were still in existence.

The Fifeshire Rifle Volunteers was set up in the mid-nineteenth century. Membership was associated with status, and most of the 30 members that had joined the Lochgelly branch by 1860 supplied their own uniforms, arms and horses. The initial ground rules drawn up for the volunteers betrayed a certain fear about just what these amateurs would get up to. Members could be fined for discharging rifles accidentally or drawing swords or bayonets in a threatening manner. Caution was justified since one Mr Rumgay was shot dead whilst acting as a marker (obviously too successfully) during rifle practice in 1876. He was found guilty of negligence posthumously and all charges against the man who shot him were dropped. In 1892 a two-day bazaar was held in Kirkcaldy to raise funds to build Lochgelly Drill Hall, above. Now the Town Hall, it has plaques on its frontage commemorating some of Lochgelly's eminent citizens.

Station Road, Lochgelly.

Peter Leslie, Lochgelly soldier and poet, was a local hero of the mid-1800s. He wrote articles for Fife newspapers from abroad which were later published as an autobiography under the pen name of Pinder. Pinder doesn't seem to have been the most dedicated of soldiers, his writings often concentrating on the important business of wooing 'sweet, romantic, girl[s]' without getting trapped by them. 'Courtship,' Pinder counsels us, 'is bliss, but matrimony often turns out a blister.' Early marriage was positively discouraged by the armed forces because it led to men acquiring dependants in the form of spouses and children. In some regiments a man could apply to get married only after seven years service, and then only if no more than 7% of its members were married already. This contributed to the widespread use of prostitutes, and the armed forces were continually plagued by venereal disease. The Contagious Diseases Acts of 1866-1869 introduced compulsory medical examinations for suspected prostitutes 'simply and solely in the hope of producing good health in the army and navy', according to the Marquis of Hartington.

Auchterderran Road, Lochgelly

Auchterderran Road is named after the parish of which Lochgelly used to be part. The single storey houses on the left (most of which have been demolished) were owned by the Lochgelly Iron and Coal Company. The cafe at the corner of Station Road and Auchterderran Road has been owned by the Macari family since the early 1970s. Former owners include the Fortes, who had the premises split into a chip shop and an ice-cream shop. The family also installed a billiard table which made the cafe popular with local boys and miners after their days' shift.

The motion to close Lochgelly Public School was carried by one vote in 1964. Lochgelly Town Council had written to its district education committee pointing out the poor conditions at the school and asking what its future plans for Lochgelly were. The answer it got was a little more than it bargained for. Since the public school had just 200 pupils it was considered more sensible to transfer Lochgelly's pupils to new schools in Ballingry and Auchterderran rather than upgrade the old one. Modernisation had taken place at Auchterderran because the NCB had predicted wrongly that Bowhill Pit would expand to employ 3,000 men. Even though plans were afoot to convert the Public School into a technical college money alone would not make it a good educational institution; the numbers were too low to offer the variety of courses available elsewhere.

Station Road, pictured at the steep bend near Launcherhead Road. The building in the distance on the right was once the Roman Catholic School, which originally had the RC iron church as its neighbour.

The winding gear in the background belonged to the Nellie Pit. In the nineteenth century railways became an integral part of developing industries, which frequently couldn't reach their markets without them; passenger traffic was often an afterthought. The Thornton to Stirling line, which provided Lochgelly with its first station, was laid in the late 1840s in tandem with development of the town's iron works. A railway had been proposed ten years earlier to transport lime and coal from Lochgelly to Inverkeithing for export, but the project never came to fruition. Stationhead Row was built in the mid-nineteenth century, its first occupiers the navvies who were engaged on the railway. An old story concerns Miss Fenton, teacher at Flockhouse School, who arrived at Lochgelly Station late one night in pitch darkness. She didn't notice that the train had overrun the station and stepped off the station bridge instead of the platform. According to local legend her billowing, crinoline skirt saved her from instant death.

Station Road. Lochgelly.

The fence in the left foreground belonged to a house built c.1860. Living in it in later years meant putting up with two hazards, both of them life-threatening. With the advent of motor cars and trams in the early twentieth century, the fence was smashed several times by vehicles losing control at the sharp bend near Launcherhead Road. Residents learned to be wary of standing near the window of the front room when buses were due to pass by. In addition, the house was built over an old pit shaft and began to suffer from an infiltration of the insidious black damp, the lethal gas which killed many miners underground. When the Coal Board was called in to conduct tests the reading was so strong that the family living there were advised to move out that very day. Lochgelly Gas Works stood behind the telegraph pole to the right.

Motion Street was named after Lochgelly Town Provost Willie Motion. The shop on the right was established as a paper shop by a local businessman and has now been extended into a superstore.

The view down The Avenue, formerly the road to Kirkcaldy, with the public park to the left. The Lochgelly Estate was bought by Sir Gilbert Elliott, whose son, Gilbert, became the first Lord Minto; this is how Minto Lodge, Cottages and House acquired their names. Sir Gilbert was extremely popular with the Lochgelly locals, acquiring the nickname 'Gibbie wi' the Gowden Garters' on account of his generosity. He apparently had villagers over to his mansion house and stood them drinks in the local pubs. Previous to this the estates had been owned by the Boswell family and, before that, by the Monastery of Inchcolm. In 1822 Sir Alex Boswell was killed by Stuart Dunearn at Orrock Quarry near Lochgelly, in what was the last duel in Scotland.

The original Minto House (also known as Lochgelly House) was a thatched abode, built by Lord Minto's family. This house was subsequently built on its site. In the 1840s it was occupied by Mr John Henderson of the Lochgelly Colliery and after that by the Minto family. The last member of the Elliot family to live there was Hugh Elliot in the 1880s, editor of the *Edinburgh Review* and credited with the dubious honour of having written the folk song 'My Sheep I Neglected/ I Broke My Sheep Hook'. Local councillor Mungo Johnston converted the house into a hotel in the late sixties. It has since been demolished.

Minto Cottages, Lochgelly.

Minto Cottages were at Brigghills; the Minto/Brigghills colliery is in the background on the right. The cottages were far from the centre of town off the Auchterderran Road and although they are marked on a 1920s map they have since disappeared. The house at the end of the road was the colliery manager's.

This rural idyll looks a million miles from industrial Lochgelly, but actually has connections with Glencraig, a nearby mining village. There is a theory that the name Glencraig derived from Clunecraig and came into being when the estates of Contal, the Clune, Inchgall and Templeland were joined. In the 1790s agriculture was still important to Lochgelly's economy; the village's main exports were the black cattle that were bred in the parish and their dairy products. Farming techniques became more efficient as time went by, and in the nineteenth century one minister noted approvingly that the recent rise in rents had encouraged the husbandmen to work hard and improve their livings. Farmers still had problems to contend with, though, such as Lochgelly's bad roads. Those to the north were inaccessible over the winter months meaning that farmers couldn't reach more distant markets and had to sell their goods at reduced prices at home instead.

The "Business Centre" Glencraig

Lochgelly served as an entertainment and shopping centre for the cluster of mining villages that grew up around it. Sir John Wilson bought the Glencraig estate in 1894 when he was chairman of the Wilson's and Clyde Coal Company. The company had sunk two pits by the following year, and additional pits were soon in operation at the nearby East and West Crosshill estates. Glencraig village grew around the colliery and was inhabited by incomers from Lanarkshire and Ayrshire. It quickly gained a reputation as being very rough, but this did nothing to hinder its success – at one point it was employing almost 1,600 miners. Over the following years the company continued to expand, opening pits at Lethans and buying the Saline Valley Colliery. When the pits finally closed in the sixties there was no other industry to take their place in this isolated one-trick town. Its population left to find work elsewhere, the rows fell into disrepair and by the 1970s all that was left was the Institute. The shop nearest the camera on the left was Chas. Barclay's chemist's.

The pokey-hat tenement on the right once housed a baker's shop. The Institute burned down a few years ago, and the site is now a grubby wasteland currently being transformed by a building development. In the past there was some confusion about whether Glencraig was officially part of Lochgelly or not since, initially, it wasn't recognised as a destination by the post office. The writer of the postcard on the opposite page explained the situation to her friend: 'Dear Ada, I forgot to mention that in your last letter you forgot to put 'By Lochgelly', and it was marked by the Post Office authorities ' Try Lochgelly'. You see it is such a small place that nobody knows where Glencraig is . . .'

Glencraig House has long since been demolished. In addition to competition from gas, electricity and nuclear power, mechanisation played a large part in the downfall of conventional mining. Belt conveyers had replaced the man-handled hutch system for transporting coal out of the pit by the 1930s and mechanised coal cutting also took its toll on the number of men required to work Lochgelly's mines. By the mid-1960s eighteen men with advanced coal cutting and loading equipment could do a job over three shifts which would formerly have taken 300. Conversely the *cost* of running this equipment was so great that the pits could not afford to be idle.

Public Park and Jenny Gray Pit, Lochgelly

The Jenny Gray pit, in the background of this picture, closed in 1959 after 105 years of operation. Mining had been carried out in the area for longer than that, however, since centuries-old workings were discovered in the vicinity when underground surveying took place in the 1900s. 350 men worked the pit's last day and the NCB claimed to have found alternative employment for all of them. For 80 men this took the form of three month's salvage work required to wind down the pit. Others were lucky enough to be transferred to pits at Kinglassie, Brigghills and Valleyfield, although those working at the latter pit had to get up at 4.15 a.m. in the morning to get to work on time. The chimney in the distance was severely damaged by lightning in the 1930s.

Lochgelly Park, near the Jenny Gray, was opened in 1905 on what was 'a red letter day for Lochgelly', according to the Town Provost who performed the duty on behalf of Lord Minto, who was posted in India at the time. The tenements in the background, built on the former Lochgelly muir, were home to miners and known as the Happyland. In the mid-1920s the town's football club was so poor that it couldn't afford to pay close season wages and lost many of its best players. Local talent was relied upon instead, and seven members of the team hailed from the Happyland. Unfortunately, the reason LFC couldn't afford proper wages was because of their bad results. During one season, the only match in which they managed to score more than one goal was the one in which their opponents, King's Park, notched up eight! Attendances at LFC's games slumped, exacerbating the club's financial problems.

The two shafts of the Nelly Pit were originally sunk in 1878. Just eighteen years later they were abandoned and allowed to fill up with water. By 1905 they were considered to be economically viable once again and were drained, No. 1 being resunk to a far deeper level. The Nellie was still employing about 400 men in the mid-1960s and was, at that point, the last steam-winding plant in Fife.

Bowhill Colliery, in Auchterderran parish, provided an alternative source of work for Lochgelly men once their pits began to close in the sixties. When Bowhill first opened in 1895 it was part of a massive development that transformed what was formerly a principally rural district into an industrial stronghold. Miners came from Ireland, Lanarkshire and the Lothians in their droves, these incomers quickly developing a reputation for political radicalism. Bowhill was 'the industrial storm centre of the Scottish coalfields' according to one commentator. It certainly did the work-force no harm, their organisation ensuring them higher than average wages. By the mid-sixties, however, alarm bells were beginning to ring. The NCB had estimated that Bowhill's work-force would increase to 3,000, and a new school had been built in the area in anticipation of this. Instead, the number of workers dropped to 1,500, and by 1990, all the industry gone, Bowhill was the focus of a Land Renewal Project.

This is an early picture of the Brigghills (or Minto) Colliery – in later years the view of it was obscured by bings. In the 1940s part of Minto No. 2 pit earned the name 'the ghost section' on account of its dangerous solid sandstone roof. This used to creak and strain prior to off-loading chunks of itself onto the miners working below, with occasional fatalities. Folklore attributes disasters such as these to fairies or pixies annoyed by miners' whistling. In 1963 the pit was earmarked for closure, but a huge effort by the work-force to improve its profitability saved it for a time. Sadly, the following year, a natural hazard brought about its demise while it was still productive. If the right conditions occur coal can catch alight and burn underground, and this is what happened. (Sir Gilbert supposedly discovered the location of a coal seam because underground fires meant that snow always melted in its vicinity.) The damage to the Minto workings meant that the pit had to be closed down.

Scholars have suggested two possible origins for the 'gelly' in Lochgelly. The alternative to *gile*, translated as 'white and shining water', is a similar word meaning leech. The loch apparently teems with these blood-sucking worms which were formerly harvested and sold bottled in chemists' shops. Eels from the loch were once caught in a trap at Shawsmill on the Gelly Burn and despatched to London. It was fish from the loch, however, that were the cause of the infamous Boswell/Wemyss dispute of the 1500s. The two landowners had fishing rights for the loch and Wemyss, feeling that his were being encroached on by the Boswells, sent 60 armed men to build a fort on the latter's side of the loch. Boswell had to get the king to intervene to prevent blood being spilled. In the past both Lord Minto and the Wemyss family had boathouses on the loch, which was also used for skating and curling when it iced over. Some very old stones found around it are thought to belong to the old curling club which was set up in 1831. These days the loch has been given a new lease of life as a venue for the Fife Water Ski Club. A permanent clubhouse and jetty have been built to accommodate it and large crowds attend its annual competitions.

The castle pictured here is actually Inchgall Castle. It was built in 1160 by Duncan de Lochore on what was Inchgall Island, the 'island of strangers'. Throughout the thirteenth and fourteenth centuries the Lochore family was politically important in Fife, owning the parishes of Ballingry and Auchterderran. Adam de Lochore was Sheriff of Perth *c*.1230 and Thomas de Lochore was one of the members of the Parliament at Ayr which in 1315 entailed the Scottish crown on the heirs of Robert Bruce. Inchgall Castle's ruins, its fourteenth century wall within its twelfth century keep, are still standing today near the entrance to Lochore Meadows Country Park. This was developed in the late sixties as part of an early scheme to reclaim land disfigured by mining.

THE BISHOP HILL FROM GOLF COURSE, LOCHGELLY.

Lochgelly's present golf course was laid out in 1913. Other entertainments in town included bowling, quoiting, tennis and the rather exclusive curling club which had Lord Minto as a member. Bishop Hill, in the background, is the subject of local legend, not least because John Knox is reputed to have preached on its slopes. In 1852 several Lochgelly men set out to dig for gold on Bishop Hill, inspired by a letter from a local man taking part in the Australian gold rush of the time. He was convinced that deposits he'd seen at Bishop Hill were similar to those in gold mines down under and rumours of that were enough to set off gold fever in the locality. Men headed for the hill but a week of frenzied land claiming and digging turned up not one ingot of true gold. Geologists were called in and proved that whatever *had* been uncovered on the hill certainly wasn't precious metal.